For Eleanor Jane Moulding
with love from her Fairy Godmother   K.S.

Text by Elena Pasquali
Illustrations copyright © 2010 Kristina Stephenson
This edition copyright © 2010 Lion Hudson

The moral rights of the author and illustrator
have been asserted

A Lion Children's Book
an imprint of
Lion Hudson plc
Wilkinson House, Jordan Hill Road,
Oxford OX2 8DR, England
www.lionhudson.com
Paperback ISBN 978 0 7459 6918 3
Hardback ISBN 978 0 7459 6266 5

First UK edition 2010
1 3 5 7 9 10 8 6 4 2
First US edition 2011
1 3 5 7 9 10 8 6 4 2 0

A catalogue record for this book is available
from the British Library

Typeset in 15/25 Palatino
Printed in China June 2011 (manufacturer LH06)

Distributed by:
UK: Marston Book Services Ltd, PO Box 269, Abingdon, Oxon OX14 4YN
USA: Trafalgar Square Publishing, 814 N Franklin Street, Chicago, IL 60610
USA Christian Market: Kregel Publications, PO Box 2607, Grand Rapids, MI 49501

Child
of
Bethlehem

Elena Pasquali

Illustrated by
Kristina Stephenson

LION
CHILDREN'S

All throughout Nazareth, children were playing,
filling the streets with laughter and noise.

But Mary was older… and soon to be married.
She tiptoed on by to daydream alone.

But there, in the orchard, was someone… or was there?
There – where the petals were drifting like snow.
"Good news," said the angel. "For you have been chosen –
to bear God's Son, Jesus: the king of the world."

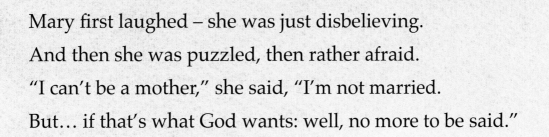

Mary first laughed – she was just disbelieving.

And then she was puzzled, then rather afraid.

"I can't be a mother," she said, "I'm not married.

But… if that's what God wants: well, no more to be said."

Soon throughout Nazareth, children were whispering.
The news about Mary had spread far and wide.

And Joseph, her husband-to-be, drooped so sadly:
"The baby's not mine; we must split up," he sighed.

That night, in the moonlight, the wind softly whispered.
An angel said, "Joseph – you're God's chosen one.
Yes, truly, you're chosen to look after Mary…
And chosen to look after God's precious Son."

The morning brought blue skies and birdsong and flowers,
the sun shining down from the heavens above.
The children came peeking and giggled with glee
to see Mary and Joseph were still so in love.

Too soon, it was time to start out on a journey –
the many long miles to Bethlehem town.
"It's all to do with what the emperor has ordered,"
said Joseph. His face was creased into a frown.

All down the road, there were families and children:
some walking, some riding – all making their way
to put their names down on the emperor's great list,
so that he could work out how much tax they should pay.

When Mary and Joseph came into the town,
they were certain there would be somewhere to stay.
They found every room in the town had been taken.
The children just watched them, in utter dismay.

"I know," said a boy, "where
there's room in a stable."

"I know," said his sister,
"where we can fetch hay."

"It's nice," said the children, "and nobody minds –
it's the not-really-secret place where we play."

There, Mary and Joseph sat down, worn and weary.
The sky turned to night and the silver stars shone.
With the ox quietly munching, the ass gently blinking,
Mary gave birth to her dear little son.

Out on the hillside, the shepherds were watching
as night's shadows spread from the east to the west.
Their sheep were all safe in a low stone-walled fold.
It was time for a fire, for some laughter, some rest.

As they sat, high above them the bright stars were shining,
drifting their way through the ocean of sky.
"Look… there's a star falling: see its tail like bright embers!"
All at once light came dazzling from heaven on high.

"Don't be scared," laughed the angel. "There's wonderful news
of a child, newly born, as from heaven above.
He brings wisdom and healing, forgiveness and friendship,
a pathway to peace and a promise of love."

Through the sky rang the cry: "Praise to God! Alleluia!"
as thousands of angels all burst into song,
to tell of the child God had sent to the earth
to banish all sorrows and right every wrong.

ar away to the east, some wise men had been watching
the night sky. For years they had mapped every star.
They knew each one's rising, they knew each one's setting;
they knew which were close and which shone from afar.

They had been wise to the sudden appearance
of a star that shone bright like a mighty king's crown.
"The sign of a king," they agreed. "We must choose gifts
and seek him and humbly bow down."

They journeyed at night, by the royal star's shining,
and children peeped out as the camels strode by –

on quiet country roads and down moonlit streets.
They all saw the star, and they all wondered why.

The shepherds came seeking, believing the angels.
The wise men were guided by light from above.
And the children just knew that the child in the manger
was newborn from heaven…

... they gave him their love.